ON GRANDDADDY'S FARM

by Thomas B. Allen

ALFRED A. KNOPF ✦ NEW YORK

THIS IS A BORZOI BOOK
PUBLISHED BY ALFRED A. KNOPF, INC.

Manufactured in Singapore
Book design by Elizabeth Hardie

2 4 6 8 0 9 7 5 3 1

Library of Congress Cataloging-in-Publication Data
Allen, Tom. On Granddaddy's Farm / by Thomas B. Allen.
p. cm. Summary: The author relates events from the
1930s, when he and his cousins spent summers on their
grandparents' farm in the hills of Tennessee.
ISBN 0-394-89613-0   ISBN 0-394-99613-5 (lib. bdg.)
1. Farm life—Tennessee—Juvenile literature.
2. Grandparents—Juvenile literature.
[1. Farm life—Tennessee. 2. Grandparents.]
I. Title S519.A45 1989 630'.9768—do19 88-23374

For Louise "Priss" McCallum
and
Dr. Benjamin Allen Shelton

In fond memory
of
Granny and Granddaddy

Over a bridge and down a tree-lined lane was Granddaddy's farm. It was there, in the rolling hills of middle Tennessee, that my cousins Priss and Ben Allen and I spent the summers.

Granddaddy was a brakeman for the L&N railroad and rode in the red caboose at the end of a long freight train. He worked the Nashville to Montgomery run and was away four days at a time.

Before he left the farm, he made sure that we three cousins knew what chores needed to be done while he was gone. We pumped water for the animals and weeded the vegetable garden. We fetched coal from the coal shed for Granny's stove and hauled water to the house from the dug well. Once we were entrusted with the job of hitching Old Mary, the big white draft horse, to the turning plow to cut a firebreak around the barn. A dry spell had left the ground so hard that one of us had to ride the plow to make it dig down into the packed earth.

Our little granny put in a full day baking and cooking, doing the wash, and taking care of the chickens and the garden. She also made sure that we cousins were well fed and well behaved and got our chores done.

After chores there was time for fun.
One day Ben Allen dared me onto a
yearling mule that had never had
anything on his back before. When
that mule felt me there, he started
bucking and running around like crazy.
I whooped and hollered like a rodeo
rider as I hung on to his mane, while
Priss and Ben Allen laughed till they
cried. Granny, hearing the ruckus,
came rushing out of the house. "Tom
Burt, you get off that mule right
now!" she yelled. The little mule gave
one enormous buck and flipped me
right into a thornbush.

The railroad yards weren't far from the farm, and when Granddaddy's train came through the cut, headed for home, the engineer gave a long pull on the whistle cord, followed by three shorts, to let the families know they were back. We knew it wouldn't be long before Granddaddy would be coming down the lane, his empty dinner basket riding lightly on his arm.

My cousins and I ran to meet him at the gate. Granny stood on the front porch, smiling and wiping her hands on her apron as if to say, "Yes, we're still here and everything's just fine."

After supper Granny and Granddaddy settled into their rockers on the porch to talk and enjoy the soft summer evening. Priss, Ben Allen, and I played outside till dark, shooting a scuffed-up basketball at the peach basket nailed above the car-shed door. We hoped Granny wouldn't tell about the yearling mule or any other trouble we'd gotten into.

We woke up every morning before dawn to the smell of biscuits baking and bacon frying. After a big breakfast we'd report to Granddaddy to get the day's assignment. I liked it best when it was a big job that needed doing, like bringing in the hay. It seemed more important than just doing chores.

After the hay was mowed and raked into windrows, we cousins piled it into stacks that Granddaddy tossed onto the wagon with one swoop of his pitchfork. It was hot work. Granny made several trips to the fields with a bucket of cool well water to quench our thirst. She always had something kind to say about our good work.

But for Priss, Ben Allen, and me the best part came after the hay was baled and stacked in the hayloft. We built a tunnel with the hay bales that we crawled through and then jumped from the loft into the straw piled below, again and again. We got covered with hay dust inside and out, but we did it anyway. The fun was worth the itching and sneezing.

Then Granny gave us a bar of
fresh-smelling homemade soap to take
down to the "blue hole" in Mill Creek.
We hung our clothes on a tree limb
and swam the dirt and dust away.

Sunday was the one day of the week when no work was done on Granddaddy's farm. After church more cousins and aunts and uncles came for Sunday dinner. All the cousins played baseball before dinner and took turns cranking the ice cream freezer. No matter how much ham and chicken and beans and potatoes and biscuits and tomatoes we ate, there was always room for homemade ice cream and Aunt Ruth's angel food cake.

Late in the afternoon the aunts
and uncles and all the other cousins
said their good-byes and drove off
with everybody waving until the cars
were out of sight. Half filled with
excitement but half empty too, Priss,
Ben Allen, and I looked for something
to do to help level out those feelings.
We went out behind the smokehouse
to the horseshoe pits, where the uncles
had just been, and pitched the rusty
horseshoes that had once belonged to
Old Mary.

Granddaddy liked to attend the Sunday evening church service, too, and he always invited us cousins to go with him. We hitched Old Mary to the buggy, and with a "come up" and a light slap of the reins, we were off at a trot. The church was small and plain. The benches were hard and had no backs. Granddaddy sat like a rock, listening to the words of the preacher, while we shifted and squirmed, trying to get comfortable. We were sound asleep by the time Old Mary trotted us back through the gate and up to the buggy shed.

It seemed like Granddaddy had just come home when he had to leave again for his run to Montgomery. Granny filled his basket with food for the journey. It was all homegrown or homemade: smoked ham, put-up vegetables, fresh fruit, biscuits, butter, blackberry jam, cake and pies. The basket weighed heavily on his arm as he told us cousins what chores needed to be done and reminded us to take care of Granny and the farm.

When we heard the train whistle blow, we knew that Granddaddy had swung up onto the steps of his caboose. We could hear the train move out of the yards and through the cut, the choo-choo-choo of the steam engine and the click-clack, clickety-clack of the rails quickening and blending into the steady rhythm that was the heartbeat of Granddaddy's life on the railroad.

The sound of the train became
more and more distant and, no matter
how hard we listened, was gone. The
empty silence that followed was slowly
filled with the distant "bobwhite" call
of quail, the buzzing of insects, and
the clucking of chickens. Priss, Ben
Allen, and I got right to our chores.
There was water to be pumped,
animals to be tended. We were proud
to be taking care of Granddaddy's farm.

THOMAS B. ALLEN grew up in Nashville and as a boy spent summers with his grandparents on their farm in the rolling hills of middle Tennessee. He attended Vanderbilt University and studied painting at the School of the Art Institute of Chicago. A successful artist whose work has been widely exhibited and has appeared in many national magazines, he also has achieved wide acclaim as an illustrator for children. *In Coal Country*, by Judith Hendershot, was a *New York Times* Best Illustrated Children's Book and a Boston Globe–Horn Book Honor Book for illustration in 1987. His other books include *Blackberries in the Dark*, by Mavis Jukes, and *The Adventures of Tom Sawyer* and *Huckleberry Finn*, both for the Franklin Library. He is currently Hallmark Distinguished Professor in the department of design at the University of Kansas in Lawrence, where he lives with his wife and daughter.